SCOOBY-DOO!
SPACE DISCOVERIES

TRACKING METEORS, ASTEROIDS, AND COMETS WITH VELMA

by Ailynn Collins

CAPSTONE PRESS
a capstone imprint

Published by Capstone Press, an imprint of Capstone
1710 Roe Crest Drive
North Mankato, Minnesota 56003
capstonepub.com

Library of Congress Cataloging-in-Publication Data
is available on the Library of Congress website.

ISBN: 9781669021445 (hardcover)
ISBN: 9781669021148 (paperback)
ISBN: 9781669021407 (ebook PDF)

Summary: Have you ever seen a shooting star? That's a meteor burning up
in Earth's atmosphere! Learn where you can spot meteor showers, what
meteorites look like, and what makes up a comet with science expert Velma
and the rest of the Scooby-Doo gang.

Editorial Credits
Editor: Carrie Sheely; Designer: Elyse White;
Media Researcher: Rebekah Hubstenberger;
Production Specialist: Whitney Schaefer

Image and Design Credits
Alamy: Matteo Omied, 22, REUTERS/Abdelhak Balhaki, 11 (top left); Getty
Images: Eratel, front cover (bottom right), iStock/andyKRAKOVSKI, 11 (top
middle), iStock/Bjorn Bakstad, 4-5, iStock/Ludovic Debono, 9 (bottom right),
iStock/Naeblys, front cover (background, middle right), 2-3, 30-31, iStock/
Xiong Yi, 6-7 (background), MARK GARLICK, 24 (bottom), Mark Stevenson/
Stocktrek Images, 19 (top), NASA/JPL-Caltec, 15 (bottom right), picture
alliance, 11 (middle), Space Frontiers, 23 (Halley's comet), wenbin, 13
(middle right); NASA: Dave C. Bowman, 28, Dimitri Gerondidakis, 18 (right),
JPL-Caltech/University of Arizona, 16 (bottom); Science Source: European
Space Agency, 23 (bottom left), RON MILLER, 15 (top); Shutterstock:
cddesign.co, design element (planets), Designua, 21 (comet), Forgem,
26-27 (background), graphic_titan, 7 (bottom right), Grisha Bruev, 20-21
(background), Helen Dream, 18-19 (background), Jiri Balek, 9 (top middle),
Jurik Peter, 10-11 (background), muratart, front cover (top left), Nazar
Yosyfiv, 16-17 (background), Nikta_Nikta, 27 (middle), Outer Space, back
cover (background), 1, 32, Valery Brozhinsky, 23 (background), Visual Unit,
13 (background), 24-25 (background), Zakharchuk, 8

All internet sites appearing in back matter were available
and accurate when this book was sent to press.

Table of Contents

Words in **bold** are in the glossary.

A Shooting Star

After a long day of investigating mysteries, Scooby-Doo and the gang relax outside under a clear, starry sky. Suddenly, something bright shoots across the sky.

Look, a shooting star! A space object called a meteor has entered Earth's **atmosphere**. It's burning hot!

Meaty-what? Must be a sign that it's time to eat, Scoob!

Yeah!

4

Meteors can leave a bright trail behind them as they speed along.

Scientists believe our **solar system** is about 4.6 billion years old. It is made up of the sun and everything attracted by its **gravity**. It includes the eight **planets** that **orbit** the sun and many moons.

Meteors, asteroids, comets, rocks, and dust are in our solar system too. These space objects have some things in common. But in other ways, they're very different. Asteroids are space rocks. Comets are mostly made of ice and dust.

Scientists think that some space objects were already there before our solar system. They believe others are leftovers from when the planets and stars formed.

FACT
A meteor can zip through the atmosphere at 30,000 miles (48,280 kilometers) per hour!

Chapter 1

Meteors, Meteoroids, and Meteorites

Meteoroids are sometimes called space rocks. Most meteoroids have broken off from larger objects such as asteroids, comets, or planets. The solar system is filled with them. Meteoroids can be as small as a speck of dust or as large as a gigantic boulder. They can zip through the solar system at 26 miles (42 km) per second.

As a meteoroid falls toward Earth, it enters the atmosphere. When air hits the zooming space rock, it creates **drag**. Drag causes the air around the rock to get so hot that it glows. This glow is what we see as a shooting star. The meteoroid is now called a meteor. If a meteor is brighter than the planet Venus in the sky, it's called a fireball.

Fireballs can appear blue in the night sky.

Cool! Keep your eyes peeled for fireballs, Scoob!

Fireball? Uh-uh! Sounds scary!

They can seem scary. But since they're so hot, they almost always break up completely before reaching Earth.

A Fireball and a Boom

In April 2022, a fireball above Indiana woke people from their sleep with a loud boom. When objects in Earth's atmosphere travel faster than the speed of sound, they create a shock wave. The shock wave creates a loud sound called a sonic boom. It sounds like an explosion.

As a meteor passes through the atmosphere, it often burns up and crumbles into dust. But sometimes parts of a meteor survive the burning. They land on the ground. These bits are usually less than five percent of the original rock. They're now called meteorites.

Scientists think about 48.5 tons of material from meteors falls to Earth every day. Most meteorites are no bigger than the size of a pebble. Because they're usually so small, it's hard to find them. They blend into their surroundings on Earth. Larger meteorites can be easier to find if they land in large, sandy areas or in areas with few rocks.

The heaviest meteorite found on Earth was discovered in Namibia in 1920. It is called the Hoba meteorite. It weighs 119,000 pounds (53,977 kilograms)! Because of the angle at which it flew through the atmosphere, this meteorite left no hole in the ground.

The Hoba meteorite remains in the place where it landed in Namibia.

Moon and Martian Rocks

Of the more than 50,000 meteorites that have been found, about 80 are from the moon. More than 60 are from the planet Mars. When a meteoroid hits the moon, pieces fly off. Pieces of Mars break off in the same way. Sometimes these pieces make it into Earth's atmosphere.

Martian meteorite

How can you tell if what you find is a meteorite? I want to find one!

You follow the clues, of course! One clue can be the rock's color. A newly fallen meteorite might be black and shiny. An older one is likely to be rusty brown. If a new meteorite falls, it might smell like sulfur.

I'm on it!

People who hunt for meteorites look for many features to know if a rock is a meteorite. They look at a rock's shape. Meteorites often have an irregular shape. They're rarely round, but they may have rounded corners.

A meteorite often contains iron or nickel. This means it would be magnetic. If you hover a magnet over it, the meteorite would be attracted to it. The metals in a meteorite also often make it quite heavy for its size.

Many meteorites have dents in them that look like thumbprints pressed into clay. These dents are called regmaglypts. Meteorites can have thin streaks created by their once-melted crust too. These are called flow lines.

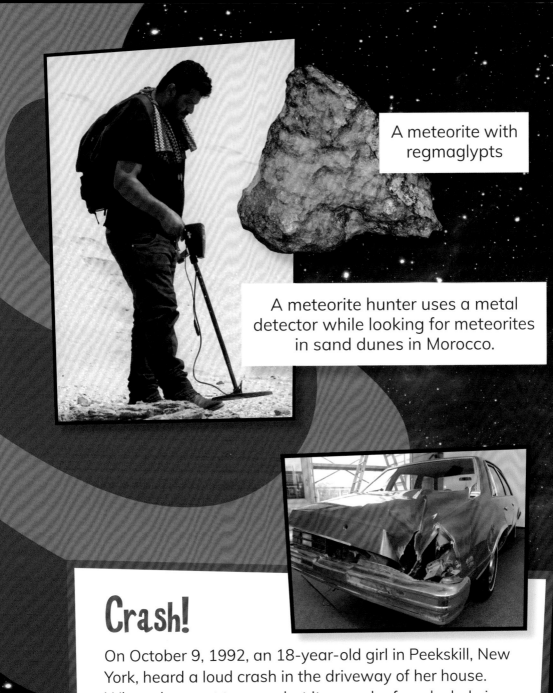

A meteorite with regmaglypts

A meteorite hunter uses a metal detector while looking for meteorites in sand dunes in Morocco.

Crash!

On October 9, 1992, an 18-year-old girl in Peekskill, New York, heard a loud crash in the driveway of her house. When she went to see what it was, she found a hole in the back of her car and another hole underneath in the ground. A meteorite had fallen right through her car! The meteorite was named Peekskill after the town where it fell.

Look over there! Many meteors!

That's a meteor shower! It happens when many meteors appear in the sky at once. It's so beautiful!

Hey! Imagine if those were Scooby snacks falling from the sky, Scoob!

Delicious!

Meteor showers are named after nearby constellations. A constellation is a group of stars. People join these stars together to make a picture. The constellation is named after the picture the stars make.

Meteor showers appear in the sky regularly. You can see one almost every month. The most well-known shower is the Perseid shower. It appears in the sky every August in the Northern **Hemisphere**. Stargazers can see 50 to 100 meteors an hour.

The Eta Aquarid meteor shower is best seen in the Southern Hemisphere in late April to May. People who live near the **equator** can also view it. About 30 meteors can be seen per hour. The meteors in this shower are known for traveling fast. They move at about 148,000 miles (238,183 km) per hour. Because of their speed, they can leave long glowing tails, or trains, behind them.

The Geminid meteor shower over Mongolia, China, in 2021

FACT

The Geminid shower in December is one of the most active meteor showers each year. People in the Northern Hemisphere can see up to 120 meteors an hour!

Chapter 2

Asteroids All Around

An asteroid is a rocky object that orbits the sun. The bigger ones are sometimes called minor or dwarf planets.

Most asteroids are made of rock and clay. These have been around the longest in the solar system. Others are made of metals such as nickel and iron.

Scientists believe asteroids are the rocky leftovers from when the planets in our solar system formed.

Speaking of leftovers, do we have any in the fridge? I'm hungry!

Reah!

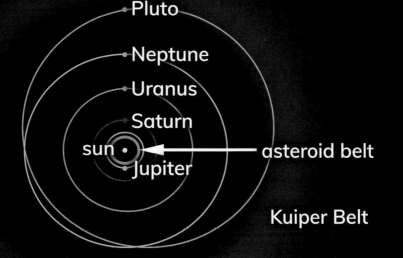

Pluto
Neptune
Uranus
Saturn
sun ◦ ◄———————— asteroid belt
Jupiter

Kuiper Belt

The U.S. space agency, NASA, estimates there are 1,113,527 asteroids in our solar system. Most asteroids are orbiting the sun between Mars and Jupiter in the asteroid belt. Others are floating around in the Kuiper Belt farther away near the dwarf planet Pluto.

Asteroids can be as large as a small planet. Vesta is the largest known asteroid. It is about 330 miles (530 km) wide. Smaller asteroids are less than 33 feet (10 meters) wide.

Vesta has large craters. Scientists believe that Vesta may have been hit by as many as 300 smaller asteroids over the last 3.5 billion years.

Asteroids that pass close by Earth are called Near-Earth Objects (NEOs). If they come closer into the orbital path of Earth around the sun, they're called Earth-crossing asteroids.

Scientists keep an eye on the asteroids that fly close to Earth. They want to know if Earth is at risk of being hit. They try to learn how close the asteroids will come to our planet. Scientists believe that 28,000 asteroids have passed close by Earth. New and better telescopes will help scientists study these asteroids. NASA is planning to launch a heat-seeking telescope called NEO Surveyor into space in 2026. It will watch for NEOs that could be dangerous to Earth.

artwork of how the NEO Surveyor may look in space

Ruh-roh!

I know this sounds scary, Scooby! But there's not an asteroid that poses a major risk of hitting Earth in the next 100 years. And scientists are always planning new ways to keep us safe.

Phew!

A Mask on an Asteroid?

In 2020, an astronomer at the Arecibo observatory in Puerto Rico saw that an asteroid passing by Earth looked like it was wearing a face mask. Scientists believe that features such as hills and ridges likely made it look like it was wearing the mask.

Scientists are very interested in studying asteroids. Their work can help us understand how planets formed. Asteroids may also contain metals that could be very valuable on Earth. Companies want to know if asteroids can be mined. But first, people have to be able to land safely on an asteroid.

Several space agencies from around the world have sent spacecraft to photograph or land on asteroids. Some have even brought back samples.

NASA's OSIRIS-REx traveled to the asteroid Bennu in 2018. Bennu passes by Earth every six years. It's about as wide as the Empire State Building in New York is tall. OSIRIS-REx collected samples of the asteroid in 2020, and the craft began its journey back to Earth.

OSIRIS-REx at Cape Canaveral Air Force Station

People might be able to travel to the asteroid belt to mine asteroids someday.

Mining asteroids poses several challenges. Asteroids spin. And there's very little gravity in space. Everything—including the people—would need to be anchored to the surface. Otherwise they would float away.

Zoinks! Like, never to be seen again! No thanks. I'll keep my feet firmly planted on good ole Earth's ground!

Sounds like they need to make a plan!

Chapter 3

Snowballs in Space

Comets are like snowballs of frozen gases, rock, and dust in space. Scientists think they're the oldest objects to exist in our solar system.

Comets orbit the sun, each with its own path. Every time a comet gets close to the sun, the ice in it melts a little. The comet then releases some of its dust and gases. This creates a cloud called a coma. It can be as wide as 50,000 miles (80,468 km).

A solid nucleus is in the middle of a comet. When light from the sun hits the dust in the cloud, the nucleus glows. The nucleus of a comet is usually less than 6 miles (10 km) wide.

A comet also has a bright tail of gas and dust. The tail can stretch more than 600,000 miles (965,600 km) long. Some comets have two tails. A white tail is made of dust, while a blue one is made of electrically charged **molecules**.

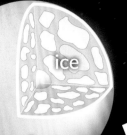

tail

coma

nucleus

ice

sunlight

STRUCTURE OF A COMET

Scientists think comets come from a faraway place in our solar system called the Oort cloud. They think it's a big shell made of icy space objects. But scientists don't know much about it because no one has ever actually seen it—even with telescopes.

Sounds like a mystery to solve!

It is! But the cloud is hard to study because it's so far away.

There are probably billions of comets in the solar system, but scientists have counted about 3,700. Some comets have lit up the sky and given people a magnificent show. In 1976, Comet West was so bright that people could take photos of its tails.

Comet West

The most famous comet is probably Halley's Comet. People have reported seeing it since ancient times. This comet can be seen from Earth once every 75 to 76 years. It last zoomed brightly across the sky in 1986. The next time we see Halley's Comet will be in 2061.

In 2011, Comet Lovejoy was clearly seen in the night sky. The comet traveled very close to the sun. Scientists expected it to completely break up. But it survived its trip through the sun's atmosphere.

Halley's Comet

When spacecraft took pictures of Halley's Comet in 1986, scientists got a big surprise! The nucleus is not round. It's shaped like a big peanut shell!

nucleus of Halley's Comet

Peanuts? Yum!

Each comet has a different length of orbit around the sun. The comet Swift-Tuttle takes 133 years to go around the sun once. Comet Giacobini-Zinner takes only 6.59 years. Comet Thatcher takes 415 years.

But not all comets orbit the sun. In 1993, scientists discovered the comet Shoemaker-Levy 9 orbiting the planet Jupiter. It was torn into several pieces that were caught in Jupiter's gravity.

On July 16, 1994, scientists watched a rare event. Fragments of the comet crashed into Jupiter with a force of 300 million **atomic bombs**. Giant plumes up to 1,900 miles (3,058 km) high rose up from the planet. The atmosphere grew as hot as 71,000 degrees Fahrenheit (39,427 degrees Celsius). The crash left dark scars on Jupiter's cloud tops for a while. Eventually, the planet's winds blew them all away.

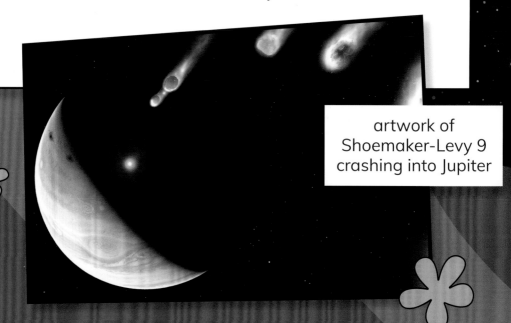

artwork of Shoemaker-Levy 9 crashing into Jupiter

Like, poof! And the scars are gone!

Yeah, just like Shaggy and Scooby's s'mores!

The scars blew away because they were made of impact debris. Scientists were able to learn about Jupiter's atmosphere by studying how the scars disappeared.

FACT

Astronomer Carolyn Shoemaker helped to discover the Shoemaker-Levy 9 comet in 1993. She discovered a record-breaking 32 new comets in her lifetime.

Chapter 4

Tracking Space Objects

Throughout history, space rocks have hit Earth. Most are so small we barely even notice them. Some are big enough to hold in your hand. However, a few space objects have affected life on Earth.

In 1908, a meteor exploded over the Tunguska River in Russia. It flattened a large forest. But the explosion was so far away from people that no one was hurt.

In 2013, a meteor the size of a building flew through the atmosphere. It broke apart above Chelyabinsk in Russia. It caused a huge shock wave that shattered windows and knocked down parts of buildings. About 1,600 people were hurt.

In 2022, an asteroid crashed just north of Iceland. It was about the size of a refrigerator, and it fell mostly into the ocean. Luckily, no one was hurt.

For an instant, the flash from the meteor that broke apart over Chelyabinsk was brighter than the sun.

The meteor that broke apart above Chelyabinsk in 2013 left a long debris trail in the sky.

FACT

About 65 million years ago, scientists believe a large asteroid crashed into Earth, killing all the dinosaurs.

Today, several organizations keep an eye on Near-Earth Objects. One is the Center for Near Earth Object Studies (CNEOS). Scientists there try to find out the orbits of objects that look like they might fly close to Earth.

In November 2021, NASA launched a spacecraft called DART (Double Asteroid Redirection Test). Scientists wanted to see if they could change an asteroid's path by crashing another object into it.

The command team monitors DART as it hits Dimorphos.

On September 26, 2022, NASA crashed DART into the asteroid Dimorphos. Scientists watched Dimorphos using telescopes and found the impact did change the asteroid's orbit. This method could help protect Earth from large incoming asteroids in the future.

Wouldn't it be exciting to be a space scientist and help keep Earth safe? Count me in!

Can we eat while we watch for asteroids? Then sure!

Hey! Do you know why asteroids are vegetarians? Because they aren't meteors.

Hee-hee. Scooby-Dooby-Doo!

Glossary

atmosphere (AT-muhss-fihr)—the layer of gases that surrounds some planets, dwarf planets, and moons

atomic bomb (uh-TOM-ik BOM)—a weapon that uses nuclear power to create massive destruction

drag (DRAG)—the force that resists the motion of an object moving through the air

equator (i-KWAY-tuhr)—an imaginary line around the middle of Earth

gravity (GRAV-uh-tee)—a force that pulls objects together

hemisphere (HEM-uhss-fihr)—one half of Earth; the equator divides Earth into northern and southern hemispheres

meteoroid (MEE-tee-uhr-oid)—a rocky or metallic chunk of matter traveling through space

molecule (MOL-uh-kyool)—the smallest part of an element that can exist and still keep the characteristics of the element

orbit (OR-bit)—to travel around an object in space; an orbit is also the path an object follows while circling an object in space

planet (PLAN-it)—a large object that moves around a star; Earth is a planet

solar system (SOH-lur SISS-tuhm)—the sun and all the planets, moons, comets, and smaller bodies orbiting it

Read More

Hulick, Kathryn. *Field Guides for Kids: The Night Sky.* Abdo Publishing: North Mankato, MN, 2022.

Lowery, Mike. *Everything Awesome About Space and Other Galactic Facts.* Orchard Books: New York, 2021.

Orr, Tamra B. *Space Discoveries.* Capstone: North Mankato, MN, 2019.

Internet Sites

NASA Kids' Club
nasa.gov/kidsclub/index.html

NASA Space Place: What Is a Comet?
spaceplace.nasa.gov/comets/en

National Geographic Kids: Asteroids
kids.nationalgeographic.com/space/article/asteroids

Index

About the Author

Ailynn Collins has written many books for children. Science and space are among her favorite subjects. She has an MFA in writing for Children and Young Adults from Hamline University and has spent many years as a teacher. She lives outside Seattle with her family and five dogs.